How To Stop Being A Toxic Husband

Introduction

You, here, reading about how not to be a toxic husband. *Why?*

It could be that your partner pointed it out, or maybe you did notice or feel like you were. Also, it could be that your marriage is not healthy, and you are taking the step to become a better partner. Better yet, you could be getting married, and you just want to make sure you'll be a great partner.

It really doesn't matter what your reason is. What matters is that you want to be a better person in your marriage. It takes courage to admit or recognize that it could be you and not the other person who is being toxic. It is admirable to take the initiative to make sure that you are a good partner for the sake of both you and your partner's mental and emotional health.

Non-toxic people create a healthy environment for a happy and healthy marriage to grow and thrive. Taking the step to change or avoid some toxic behaviors is the first step towards having that great marriage that you have always wished for.

This book has been written for any man who intends to be a good, nurturing, and supportive husband to their partner. Remember, a man leads, and a leader needs to set the pace.

Do not wait for the other person to step up and become better; you need to focus on becoming better yourself.

Read on to learn how not to be a toxic husband. It's your investment for a healthy relationship because when you become a healthy and great partner, you set a positive environment to communicate, share, nurture and walk together. It also brings out the best in the other person.

You want this, right?

It's what everyone has in mind when they get married. Let's get started and learn just how to be the best husband and play a part in having the marriage of your dreams!

Table of Contents

Introduction 2

Chapter 1: Is Your Marriage Toxic? 6

Signs That Your Marriage Has Gone Toxic 9

Chapter 2: It's Not Always Them – Sometimes, It's You 25

How to Identify Your Toxic Behaviors 27

Chapter 3: Toxic Actions and Behaviors That Can Be Confused for or Masqueraded as Love – Don't Do It! 38

Allan and Emma 39

Toxic Actions Confused As Love 43

Chapter 4: How To Stop Being a Toxic Husband and Become a Healthy and Loving Spouse 61

Conclusion 92

Chapter 1: Is Your Marriage Toxic?

Do you feel like your relationship is not like it used to be?

Are you unhappy, and does it feel like you are straining to show or experience love?

What could be ailing your marriage?

Sometimes there might just be some unresolved issues that you need to talk about soberly. Other times, there are behavioral issues by either or both partners that need to be corrected. And sometimes, it may be because your relationship has gotten toxic because of all the above and more.

Toxic?

What comes to mind when you hear the word toxic?

This is a word associated with anything harmful that is believed to cause serious harm – something that is poisonous. Whenever this word is attached to a person, a thing, or an experience, it naturally elicits fear, hatred, and loathing reactions. It is something you definitely want to stay away from for your safety or health.

Yes, I know you have heard the word before regarding relationships and marriages. That's probably why you are here because you know 'toxicity' is the leading destroyer of marriages.

These days, a relationship fails, and people are quick to cite 'it was toxic' as the reason it had to end. Today, 'toxic' has become the tag for any strife or misunderstanding in marriage.

Many people, even some marriage counselors, will tell you, "If it's toxic, you have to leave before it harms you."

As a result, we have many people jumping out of marriages for trivial reasons in the name of toxic.

But the questions that beg are,

Do we really know what a relationship that has reached levels of toxic looks like?

Is this the appropriate tag for the issues in our relationships or are we just jumping on a popular word?

Either way, you are here because you feel there is something off with your marriage.

Maybe it doesn't feel great, and you don't feel as you used to about the union or your partner.

What's the problem?

Can you say that your marriage is toxic, or are there just a few misunderstandings that you may be too proud to sit down and discuss?

Just like the proverbial frog in a pot that couldn't tell whether the water was warming or boiling until it was getting cooked, it's hard to tell when you are in the midst of a marriage conflict that has gone from normal to toxic.

It can be hard to tell when the playful bite meant to tickle starts to break the skin. You may not see it, maybe because you are so hopeful that things will work out, or you are ignorant of your feelings about certain things.

Whether you choose to acknowledge, assume or ignore, these signs indicate that a relationship has gotten to an unhealthy curve, and if not checked, it will be nose-diving to the bottom of a dark pit.

Signs That Your Marriage Has Gone Toxic

Discussed below are particular signs that your marriage is beyond 'just small issues' and has gotten to the 'toxic' level and needs a lot more attention.

1. Lack of or Change In Communication

How is communication in your household?

Are you just talking because you find yourselves in the same house, or are you communicating on an intimate level and actually connecting?

Take a moment and look closely at the state of your communication. While at it, please note that just talking is not communication. 'Just talking' can fall into either of these categories;

- *Talking At One Another*

This includes giving commands/orders or exchanging angry words. For instance, "don't come home late, again," "I want chicken for dinner," "stop dropping your dirty clothes on the floor and making me clean after you," and so on.

- *Errand Talk*

In case you are wondering what 'errand talk' is, it refers to the boring talk that couples must have about responsibilities and errands in the household. "The kids leave school in 2 hours; please remember to pick them up," "please remember to get us more lettuce and milk," "remember to invite the Anthony's."

- *Talking Across or Over One Another*

This is probably the worst and can be an indication that your marriage is already on its deathbed. When you are talking across each other, it implies that neither of you is listening to the other.

Every conversation quickly escalates and becomes a battlefield involving an exchange of insulting words, blaming, name-calling, you name it. And then no one wants or even misses to talk to the other anymore, maybe for a few days.

- *Cross-Examination*

Have you ever watched the police interrogating a suspect, the questions they ask, and how they speak even when they say that they are just having 'a chat?' That is what cross-examination looks like.

You may be talking without fighting, but this type of 'talking' is not of a partner who is genuinely interested in what the other has to say. It is not a mark of interest but a mark of someone who has something to prove and who believes themselves to be in a position of authority.

It has nothing to do with trying to understand someone better. They are asking questions either rhetorically or cross-examining to compel answers from the other person – giving them no choice but to answer.

You can tell it is cross-examination by the tone of voice used, which is primarily authoritative, and the questions asked. It is never about "How do you feel about this?" it is "do you think you should be angry about this?"

Even if it's the former question, the tone and stance of the questioner already tell you that they are not interested in your opinion. Rather, they are showing out authority – and you may need to lie about your real feelings lest your 'confession' is used against you.

Cross-examination cannot make deep and intimate conversation. It backs a spouse; it confuses, disarms, and pushes a partner into a corner. It is meant to create self-doubt and only serves to gratify the ego of the questioner. It is toxic.

In a marriage, the real definition of communication is not question and answer, the popular errand talks, the dreaded cross talking, or cross-examination. This is what you have to do because you happen to share a home with another person you don't like anymore. You do it because you have to.

You may be talking, but if the above represents the format of most of your conversations, something is wrong. It signifies a major disconnection in your marriage and is also a sign that the friendship at the root of your relationship has started to die.

You are no longer interested in each other's lives, what the other person is feeling, what they need, and what they are doing. Your partner has become just one of your homies— or an enemy you have to be content to live with.

If you feel the disconnect or change in communication and feel like you are not really in sync with each other in feelings, activities, and so on, you are not really communicating.

If you have traded deep, meaningful conversations with errand talk and commands and feel like you are not getting through to each other, there is a serious communication issue in your marriage.

Where people are not communicating, the door is open for all sorts of troubles to start creeping in; misunderstandings, full-blown conflicts, insecurities, infidelity, and so on. If you are not communicating, your marriage is not healthy.

It is a sign of the infamous 'toxic.'

2. Criticism In Its Destructive Forms

It is okay to criticize each other from time to time. However, criticism in a marriage is supposed to be healthy, meant to correct and encourage each other to become better versions of ourselves.

However, destructive criticism goes beyond correcting or voicing a concern or complaint, which happens on a case-by-case basis.

It becomes an ongoing attack, directed at the other person's character, not a behavior or a single action. It has an agenda behind it, driven by contempt mostly to make the other person feel bad about themselves and scratch their sense of worth.

When it's destructive and constant, you know, to always find fault with the other person, it causes resentment, injured self-esteem, contempt, and defensiveness, all of which are toxic to your marriage.

3. Lack of Empathy

Being selfish is a normal human characteristic. It is natural that we would want the best for ourselves and selfishly guard our interests and do things that favor us. There is nothing wrong with this, especially because it helps us protect and stand for ourselves in a world that threatens to take advantage and take everything from us.

However, selfishness has limits. If it gets into your head and it strips you of compassion and empathy towards others, then it's too little too poisonous. This kind of selfishness makes you the person who takes advantage of others and would hurt them and strip them off everything for your benefit.

Lack of empathy and compassion in a marriage is a sign that it has become poisonous. Sharing life together, you have to care about and consider the other person in every decision, action, and spoken word.

If you can't take an interest in what the other person might be experiencing, care about their feelings or even give them a listening ear, you are what they call a *narcissist*. This is a common word used these days for incredibly selfish people who lack empathy and compassion. This kind of person only sees others as existing, only to be seen, not heard, and to take orders and serve them.

Have you seen such type of behavior in your marriage?

Do you have empathy and compassion for each other, or is there someone who seems to be in authority giving orders and never caring about what the other person feels?

If yes, that's a sign that it's getting poisonous.

4. Exclusion

Are you involved in each other's lives?

Exclusion is another sign that your marriage has gotten toxic. If you seem to edge each other out of your lives, then there might be a problem.

For instance, you do not acknowledge each other to family, friends, or colleagues, never go out together, make solo vacations a norm, and do projects without involving each other; this is what exclusion looks like.

As a couple, you have to do things together. It does not have to be physically together, but the other person ought to be let in on what their partner is up to. This signifies the unity and oneness you promised each other when you got married.

Also, acknowledgment goes a long way. Imagine going to your partner's office, and a colleague asked who you were, and they said "uh, no one important" or "just a guy I know," how would that feel? Ouch!

Exclusion clearly shows that there is no true love, cherishing, or full commitment. It makes one feel left out and alone while still with a partner.

If a person who used to include you starts to exclude you, it may signify that they are disengaging from the relationship.

5. Gaslighting

This is a famous toxic behavior. It is complex as not many people really notice when they are doing the gaslighting or even experiencing it. Sometimes its purposeful manipulation but most times, it is an unconscious defense mechanism for someone who has a deep-seated need for control.

Gaslighters need to be right and have difficulty accepting that they can be wrong or capable of hurtful behaviors. This is toxic behavior that begins as a way to escape having to take responsibility for our actions or how we make other people feel.

You do it to psychologically and emotionally manipulate another person into mistrusting their emotions, judgment, and self-worth.

If you know their weaknesses, insecurities, and areas of self-doubt and use them to make them undermine their perceptions or judgment, you are gaslighting. If you do something wrong, but you won't take responsibility and apologize or make amends but instead manipulate your partner to shift blame and make them think it's their fault, then that's gaslighting.

Some gaslighting phrases look innocent, such as; "it's just your imagination," "It was never my intention," "if you had not done this, I wouldn't have done this (hurtful behavior)" "See what you made me do."

It comes out as a non-issue as gas lighters use subtle wordplay. However, this doesn't change the fact that this is psychological control and a highly damaging sign of a toxic union.

6. Walking On Eggshells

So, you are married, but you cannot speak freely about issues, whether big or small. You avoid talking about things because you are afraid that the talk may spook the other person. Important issues and also non-issues are swept under the rug because they are afraid of the other person's reaction.

For example, you cannot introduce a colleague or friend of the opposite sex in a gathering because you are afraid of what they may think. You cannot tell them that you had dinner with friends because they will not take it well. Unfortunately, they see the restaurant receipts, and you hold your breath waiting for a tantrum and accusations of cheating, lying, and so on.

7. Insecurity

Insecurities come when your body and mind sense the danger of loss, not because of anything real, but because of fear. We all desire the *occasional* reassurance of love and commitment in a relationship as it makes us feel safe— which is okay. Insecurity comes in the form of a *chronic* need for reassurance.

When we are insecure, we pressure our partners to do things in a certain way that disarms our fears. We want them to 'stop making us feel that way' while all along, it is us who are allowing ourselves to feel threatened by otherwise normal things.

For instance, when you do not want to pick a particular call, maybe because the person calling is nagging you about an issue you don't really want to talk about (it could be work-related).

This could be completely innocent. However, an insecure spouse could assume that you won't pick the call because you are probably cheating with the person on the line, and you don't want to expose yourself.

They may make a scene, cuss you out and create a fight out of this. A secure spouse will trust you and won't be bothered unless it becomes a recurring issue.

Insecurity will show up in your relationship as a fear that there may be another person. The insecure spouse will think that the other person is cheating, is thinking about being unfaithful, wants to be unfaithful or used to cheat.

The more they are reassured, the greater the insecurity gets because all this time, they are wondering 'why is she/he trying so hard to convince me?"

This becomes evidence to confirm their fears. It's destructive as you are damned whether you say anything or you don't.

Have you witnessed such a trend in your marriage?

8. Lies, Lies, Lies

In the beginning, little white lies are used to navigate the relationship and avoid some tough or uncomfortable discussions and questions. Soon after, lying becomes the only way you can navigate your relationship.

Lies can be used to manipulate the other person to do certain things that they may otherwise not agree to. They are used to avoid the day-to-day truths about the simple stuff such as why you are arriving home at midnight, or why you applied for another credit card, or if you have been speaking to your ex who just 'suddenly called.'

You begin lying about whereabouts, friends, money, chores, and the cycle continues.

The thing with lying is that it may not have immediate negative consequences because it may not be immediately revealed that all that a person has been believing is just a smokescreen of reality.

However, over time, lies build up disrespect for self and the other person as well. They become toxic even to the liar and can be very destructive.

Judging by the signs discussed above and taking a close look at your marriage and how you behave towards each other, do you find evidence that you are living in a toxic union?

If so, who is creating the toxic mess in what was a wonderful union?

Before you point fingers, please read the next chapter.

Chapter 2: It's Not Always Them – Sometimes, It's You

Who do you think is the toxic one?

Who is causing all these problems in what used to be or what you hoped would be a healthy and happy relationship?

It is probably them, right?

Oh! Isn't it easy to avoid taking responsibility and shift blame to the other person?!

How about you; have you really checked yourself?

What part have you been playing in creating that toxic situation?

In our eyes, we tend to have an impression that we are living blameless lives. We blame society, our circumstances, conditions, lack of money, and we blame our partners. When things go south, we look for external things as the cause of our problems.

It is important to understand and accept the truth that sometimes it's not them; **it's you**. The talk of 'removing the toxic person in your life' when relationships get rocky is common. But have you stopped to think that the toxic person who is jeopardizing that relationship could be you?

Having a great relationship is not only about getting rid of toxic people. You might get rid of your partner because you think it's them who are toxic. Maybe they are. However, if you are not honest about your own toxic tendencies, what good will it do you?

You may find love again, which at first feels great, but since you still got those toxic tendencies which, if you bring to a new relationship, will ruin it, just like the last one. You will be jumping from one relationship to another, searching for the 'right non-toxic person', and get frustrated for nothing because the only person who needed fixing first was you.

Yes, we are blind to our faults – it's a common human tendency. However, the faster you remove the blindfold and face your faults, the sooner you will be able to become a better man.

This is the man needed to lead a relationship in the right direction – a direction of love, understanding, support, mental and emotional health for both partners, and so on.

How to Identify Your Toxic Behaviors

It can be hard to admit that you are the problem; to admit that you have been a thorn in someone's flesh, that you have been taking more than you give, that you have been making excuses to justify your wrongs towards the other person. But it is the first big step you are making to becoming a good partner deserving of that great relationship you want.

To pinpoint your toxic traits:

- *Ask People Around You/Your Partner*

In our eyes, we are always faultless and perfect human beings. No one sees or can even acknowledge that they are villains. Even with the bad things we do, we somehow manage to make excuses to cover up the evil and justify our actions. This is why it's so hard to identify yourself as the villain in your marriage.

Do you suspect that you could be blindsided when evaluating your behavior (which we all tend to be btw)?

If you do, ask someone close to you who loves you and wants the best for you. They will tell you things about yourself that you may be missing either through ignorance or that perfect blindfold we can't help but wear.

In this case, you start by getting the opinion of your partner. Ask them to describe what kind of a person you are. Let them know that they can speak freely, without fear of offending you with some hard-to-swallow truths.

Ask questions like, "how do I treat you/people," "How do I make you feel?," "Do I make you feel loved and appreciated?," "In your opinion, what

28

kind of a person/partner am I?," "Describe my personality without trying to please me," "What do you think I should change about myself?"

This will help shed light on the type of person you really are. Also, you want to be careful that you do not become a victim of blame. But also, do not make yourself one when the truth is too bitter to accept. Take time to reflect on their words and consciously search yourself to find out the truth which is within you. The next step should help;

- *Take a Toxic Traits Personality Test*

No one is born toxic. Most of these toxic behaviors we pick up on our life's journey as we learn from the environment and situations we are exposed to and the people we interact with.

Stressful situations or pressures of life inculcate these toxic traits in people. More often than not, many are unaware of their toxic behaviors. This is where this test comes in. It helps you uncover toxic traits that you possess but which you may be unconscious of.

Answer the questions below as honestly as you can. Remember, no one is looking, so you do not have to pretend to be perfect. Bare your soul to yourself and be completely honest. This is the only way this test will help you uncover whatever toxic traits you might have.

Test

i. What person are you when you are relating with others?

> A. The master (in control, and everyone should serve and listen to you)?
>
> B. The servant (the meek one who is only a follower)?
>
> C. An equal associate (confident in their skin, no need to belittle others to feel strong or become meek to be liked)?

(As you answer this, remember that matters of social class, education, or intelligence of your associates are notwithstanding.)

ii. When you are having a conversation, what do you do most?

    A. Listen

    B. Talk about yourself

    C. Listen and share your opinions

iii. Are you always looking for the negative side of the story?

    A. Yes, I like to look at the dark side

    B. No, I am quite the optimist

C. No, I am an optimist, but I like to consider both sides, the good and the bad.

iv. Do you often have to push people to do things your way?

A. Yes, my way is the best because my standards are high

B. No, I let them do whatever works for them

C. No, I offer my opinion, but I let them choose what they would rather.

v. Would you rather tell an uncomfortable truth or lie your way out of and through a difficult situation?

A. I tell people what they want to hear, even if it means lying

B. I would rather say nothing – avoid the conversation

C. Yes, I tell the truth no matter what

vi. Do you believe that other people's goals matter, no matter how small or 'shallow' they may seem?

A. No, I think only great things should matter

B. Not when I can give them better ideas

C. Yes, everyone is on their journey, and what may seem small to me may be big to them.

vii. When someone does wrong, do you believe that telling it as it, criticizing on the spot, or using the strongest words possible to get the point through will make them do better?

A. Yes, I don't sugarcoat. I give it to them raw and real

B. Yes, sometimes someone has got to have the courage to tell them as it is

C. No, it is best first to understand where they are coming from

viii.   Do you feel a sense of triumph when you win an argument?

A. Oh yes!

B. When I am defending what's right, yes, it makes me feel powerful.

C. No, winning is never the point

ix.   Do you blame others when things go wrong?

A. Yes, its always some careless person's fault

B. Yes, if they are to blame

C. No, I understand I make mistakes too, and blaming does not bring solutions.

x. Do you often overhear negative things about yourself?

A. Yes, very often. But I don't care about the haters

B. I don't listen to what people have to say about me

C. Not really, but I am open to positive criticism

xi. How do you react when someone criticizes or confronts you?

A. I defend myself strongly

B. I walk away

C. I try to understand what could have prompted them

xii. Have you ever said bad things to someone just to make it clear who is in charge?

A. Yes, sometimes it's inevitable.

B. I don't say; I show them

C. No, I try not to use abuse or intimidate to get power

Evaluate your answers and see how many As, Bs, or Cs you got.

Getting **more than 5 As** means that you have acquired and are displaying very toxic behaviors. You are way in over your head in the swamp of toxicity and are incredibly toxic in your relationships with others.

More than 5 Bs means that you have toxicity traces but only come out as a mildly toxic individual. You are well on your way to becoming fully toxic if you don't take care.

If you have **plenty of Cs**, it is an indication that you are an individual who is making an effort to have healthy relationships with self and other people. We can say that you are pretty balanced.

Chapter 3: Toxic Actions and Behaviors That Can Be Confused for or Masqueraded as Love – Don't Do It!

I do it because I love my partner.

It is not uncommon to hear a man defend an openly toxic thing they have been doing with this statement. In their mind, they have convinced themselves that it is a 'love thing.'

They are oblivious of how negatively their behavior affects their significant other because they believe that their actions come from a place of love.

They will ignore the distress they are causing and dismiss any complaints citing, 'I do this because I love you; if I didn't, then I would not bother."

In other words, their partner should be grateful that they do these things because it shows how much they love them.

It can be assumed that the men who do this are aware that their actions are toxic. Unfortunately, a good number are not aware. They think it's a normal way for a man in love to act, and honestly, they cannot be blamed because chances are they grew up in an environment where such actions were seen in that light – and were promoted.

Allan and Emma

For example, Allan is married. He loves his wife and can never imagine his life without her. He would give anything to make sure that theirs is a happily ever after stretching to infinity. This is a good thing, isn't it?

But Allan is afraid that someone will come and cheat Emma out of their marriage. She has not given him any reason to believe that she can leave him.

However, she travels a lot for work and always has clients and colleagues calling her even when she is not working. He voiced his concern about it, but she reassured him that nothing and no one could come in between them – it's just work.

Emma works in a male-dominated field, and her work can be very demanding. She tries to separate her work and her personals. She bans people from calling her on her personal cell, but she just cannot control everyone. And there is no way she will drop a call when it's an urgent one from a client or her boss about something that's her responsibility.

About traveling, canceling all her international and regional engagements will just mean that she has to quit her job because that's where business is. Also, she cannot get Allan on board every trip because her company cannot approve of all the travel costs for two.

Allan is getting insecure by the day, even when Emma is doing everything to make sure that he feels loved, wanted, and cared for despite her busyness. He still thinks that someone will snatch Emma from him amid all this travel and work. His wife says there is nothing to worry about, but he just won't believe it.

Then Allan taps his wife's phone so that he can listen in to her calls and see all her messages – just to make sure there is no one else. He installs an app that also tracks her movements to be aware of her location at all times. He will also sneak into hotels where his wife is having meetings and check who she is with.

Now he sees things in her conversations, the usual stuff, and the inevitable weird texts from friends and admirers, from a very different perspective. He is looking at it as very inappropriate and confronts his wife about it.

He says that she entertains 'bad friends' and implies that she is cheating on him just because she is admired by others, which she has little control over.

Emma is mad; first, because he has violated her right to privacy by getting unlawful malware in her phone to access what's supposed to be personal without her permission.

Secondly, Allan is trying to control every aspect of her life by tracking and following her and monitoring her communication. He is also telling her who to talk to and who to cancel out of her life. He is accusing her of being unfaithful, which is not true. He clearly does trust her or believe in their marriage.

Suddenly her darling Allan has become this controlling, overly jealous person. He has overstepped her boundaries, and she is not taking it. Emma cannot stand to be in the same room with that man anymore. He is losing her, and he is going nuts.

When asked, 'what were you thinking, man? Emma is a wonderful woman. Why would you do that?"

He says, "I only did it because I love her so much. I don't want to lose her. If I didn't love Emma, I would not be caring about who she talks to or where she goes. I did it because I want to keep my woman."

But really, Allan, is that how a man keeps a woman?

Is being a toxic, controlling, and manipulative maniac how you show love to a woman?

Is that how you make sure she doesn't leave with someone better than you?

I don't know about you, but in my opinion, that's the way to lose a woman - forever.

Are you like Allan?

Could you have been doing something in the name of love, but it turns out it's actually a toxic behavior that is choking the life out of your relationship?

Toxic Actions Confused As Love

The following is an outline of toxic actions and behaviors that can easily be confused as love:

1. **The Need For Your Partner To Be Your 'Everything.'**

It looks like love, doesn't it?

This idea that to be in love is to be or have someone as your 'one and only,' is used to make catchy verses in love songs; 'I would give up the world to be your one and only,' 'you are my only one,' 'nobody but you.'

I mean, we like this idea, don't we? It seems like the ideal love situation.

But really, is this love?

Your partner is an independent individual with a life, needs, desires, dreams, unique personality, strengths, and faults. You are an independent individual as well, and you should have your own life, goals, dreams, and desires.

So, why would you want someone to come into your life and become your everything?

Why do we want to convert someone who has their individual life to live into 'your everything'?

This enclosed love mentality seeks to romanticize the toxic action of staking our joy, value, wellbeing, worth, and expectations of a fairytale experience on one person.

If you cannot do it yourself, don't you think it's a great burden to place it on someone else's back?

Will they live their life, handle their issues, find joy and cater for their own wellness while you expect them to do it for you too?

How will they manage it?

And if they can't or fall short, will you feel like they do not love you as you deserve?

This is a mentality that looks and feels like being deeply and deliriously in love. It is strongest during the first days of a relationship, but it can barely hold up a few months for some couples.

It breeds unhealthy dependence, neediness, insecurity, and resentment (when the other person cannot live up to expectations) in the relationship.

It sounds cute, but it definitely isn't healthy.

2. Jealousy

Many people believe that jealousy is a sign or requirement of love; if they aren't jealous, they aren't that into you.

Is there any truth to this?

Shakespeare called it the 'green-eyed monster.' It is not just a feeling; just like love, it is multi-dimensional. It involves emotions, thoughts, and behaviors that are often portrayed negatively, but some regard them as positive for some reason.

There may be no facts to support whether jealousy is good or bad for a relationship. Experts suggest that when and how people feel and express jealousy depends on who they are as a person – not on what jealousy is or isn't. The behavior, emotions, and thoughts displayed will tell you all you need to know.

Jealous people have often been perceived as unreasonable, controlling, possessive and troubled.

Experts have often linked romantic jealousy with strife and dissatisfaction in a relationship. When it enters a relationship, suspicion and conflict follow, and often it will bring pain.

Some behaviors associated with jealousy in relationships include;

- Spying on your partner

- Extreme possessiveness whereby you would not like them to be around or associate closely with anyone else,

- Controlling who they speak to or hang out with, and so on because there are people you think will take them away, etc.

Jealousy will make you incredibly unreasonable, insecure, and paranoid.

It is caused by fear. Yes, often, it's nothing more than fear. It may seem like insecurity and possessiveness but beneath this is fear. It is not meant to be perceived as bad. This is only an emotion which in this case serves to inform us that we are in danger of losing our loved one's attention and affection to someone or something.

This is not a problem, so do not beat yourself up when you are feeling a little possessive. We may feel like that from time to time when we love a person and look at all the amazing people they are around, which is normal and perhaps why some believe that jealousy is synonymous with love.

However, it becomes a problem when we dwell on, entertain, and get overly consumed by this fear, and it starts to manifest as jealousy. This fear contaminates a relationship and destroys our freedom and that of our partner as we hold them so possessively; we are literally crushing them. It distances us from the love we thought we were so fiercely preserving.

If you express your jealousy in a way that your partner can see and feel, bringing misunderstandings and unnecessary fights, then it has probably gone overboard, and it's toxic.

Jealousy that can be synonymous with love is so subtle that your partner would never really notice, and if they did, it would be so endearing that they would not complain about it. Be careful, though, when you let that subtle jealousy tag at you from time to time because the full-blown destructive kind grows from this if entertained long enough and fed with insecurities.

So, no, if you are constantly having fights or conversations about jealousy, probably because it is no longer subtle, it involves toxic actions and behaviors that are suffocating your partner. Stop defending it already.

That is not love. It is a toxic behavior you have invited into your marriage in the name of love, to kill it.

3. Being Honest About Everything

Hey, I am not telling you that little white lies here, and there are okay. If you do that, it will be the beginning of the end because you know that you will be caught eventually.

Honesty is among the top 3 admirable qualities when looking for a partner. So, what do we mean when we say that being honest about everything is a toxic trait?

Isn't this what is needed for relationships to work?

It is. You need to be honest with your partner, but sometimes you can take this honesty too far, and that's how it becomes toxic. Let me explain;

Your lady thinks that the guy who moved next door is really nice, not to mention hot - the one she found lost in the lobby and helped him find his way. In fact, he brought you cupcakes as a way to say thank you, and when he leaves, she says, 'Mmmh, honey, what do you think? Such a hunk, not to mention with a heart of gold. I like him already!'

Hey, this is 100% honest. It's the way she sees the guy for some reason. Maybe he is truly a hunk and has a good heart. She likes him, maybe as a new neighbor or well, you don't know what she means by she likes him already.

Now, tell me how you feel about her being this honest, like when she says that her new boss, a muscled hunk, favors her for some reason, and she thinks he likes her.

Well, brother, this is some information that will trigger jealousy, insecurity, and whatnot. You are going to sit there and look at that woman and wonder why the hell she thought to tell you that her new boss is hitting on her. It is going to mess up your mind and make you so paranoid! I doubt you will be as calm as you have been every time she steps out of the door.

Imagine if your partner keeps telling you stuff like this, keeping it 100% honest with you and messing with your mind. How uncomfortable will it get? My guess is too uncomfortable – and toxic.

To be honest, as hard as it is to believe, there are things about your partner or your relationship that you and your partner don't need to know. Even if you want to know and are wondering if, there are times when the best thing for your marriage is to assume ignorance or become willfully unaware.

Telling them everything, including hurtful details about things you know will hurt her, is toxic. You are honest, but how will it benefit your relationship? How will it help the other person become better or feel better?

Also, expecting them to tell you everything is a toxic trait. You don't want to press her about what she thinks about that bothersome member of your family, even when you see the 'hot' looks she gives them. She hates them and would kick them out, but she could be tolerating them for the sake of your marriage.

You don't need her to tell you about all the guys hitting on her at work or what she is speaking on the phone about with that guy from work – unless she wants to talk about it.

Leave it alone; you don't have to know everything. That is what Allan was doing – trying to know everything by accessing all his wife's conversations. He got traumatized in the process, and he lost her when she genuinely loved him and protected their relationship.

Too much honesty about the wrong, and sometimes the right, but unnecessary stuff is very toxic.

I know now you agree with me that some things are best left alone.

4. Requiring or Needing to be Taken Care of

If you ask many men, being taken care of is one of the reasons why they get married. There is nothing wrong with wanting to be taken care of – we all need that. It is a way to express love.

However, there are things in your life that you need to take care of yourself. Dumping every baggage on your back at the hands of your partner and expect them to take care of it for you, to make you feel better, is not love.

For example, you have had a bad day at work; you come home stressed and with a bad headache. To care for you, they give you some medicine for the pain and ensure that you go to a clean and fresh bed to rest. If you need to talk about it, they can give you a listening ear. This is healthy care.

But some of us have unhealthy expectations of care. You expect that your partner will drop everything and sit there all evening listening to your woes, rubbing your back, and somehow trying to fix you.

And when they don't, then they don't love you?

Maybe they had a work engagement or needed to help the kids do their homework and eat, or they had already planned to get together with some friends. Sometimes, they may also be having a bad day, just like you.

Isn't it selfish to make your loved one feel like they have to drop everything and cater to you or try to fix your world for you?

Unless they want to do it out of their free will and their emotional and mental state allows it, no one should ever be made to feel like the wellbeing of another grown-up that is independent and fully able is in their hands. It is such a heavy burden to carry, given that they have to care for themselves, and perhaps minors too, especially in a marriage setting.

Blaming your partner for your emotions and for 'not being there for you' is a subtle form of selfishness. No one can fix your emotional issues but you. When you make your partner feel responsible for how you feel and vice versa, you have invited a toxic habit that could introduce codependency and insecurity in your marriage. No, it is not love.

5. Doing Everything Together

So you get married and feeling like you are attached like Siamese twins. You cannot get enough of each other, and you want to spend every minute of the day by each other's side. You want to do every little thing together.

You know the feeling, right?

It is cute, for a while. But this is how toxic codependency is introduced to an otherwise healthy marriage. As time goes by, it becomes suffocating.

No matter how close and in love you are, personal space and time is very important. We each need time to be alone and do the things that we love without the other person on the side pretending to enjoy it. You should be able to go out there, make new friends, and discover new things alone.

This helps retain your individuality and independence – which is important to maintain even after marriage. If you are happy as an individual, you come to the marriage whole, not needing the other person to fix you or make you happy.

This is why expecting to do everything with your partner, maybe as you did initially, can be classified as a toxic trait. If you do not want the other person to have a life of their own and want to be involved in everything they do, you are simply controlling – not loving.

This behavior could be driven by insecurities, that your love is not safe if your partner is out there alone, which would not be the case if you trusted yourself and your partner.

6. Sugarcoating Issues and Not Talking About The Hard Stuff

A man comes home, beat and sad. He looks like he is carrying the weight of the world on his shoulders. His partner gets worried and wonders what could be bothering them so much. Do you know what the man says? "Everything is okay; you don't have to worry about me."

It could be that they have serious issues at work threatening their job. Maybe they lost a good friend. It could be he is worried about not making enough money to pay off the mortgage. Whatever it is, they clearly are going through a tough time. But they are lying about it and saying everything is fine, sugarcoating something that is clearly pepper.

Why are they doing this?

Because they love their partner and wouldn't like them to get hurt.

You cannot hide the hard stuff, whether personal or about your marriage, and expect that you two will just be fine.

I mean, you look like I should be really worried, but you are telling me that I shouldn't?

I got the letter from the bank about the late mortgage payments, and you are telling me everything is fine? It isn't, and this is not protection or love.

That person who married you is called a partner for a reason. They signed up to walk with you through life as you face the storms and enjoy the sunny days too. They expect to be a partner, not to live in a false bubble of safety as you fight battles, they either do not know of or which you are 'sugarcoating.' It makes one feel left out, sidelined, and like they do not have a place in your heart or marriage.

If you cannot trust them enough to be honest about the hard stuff, it feels like you have not let them in, and therefore, it becomes hard to connect.

It is frustrating to see your partner suffer, yet they cannot be honest about what is causing them the pain. It is even harder to experience negative consequences of something you did not see coming, like being locked out of your house or dealing with an illness, which your partner knew and could have prepared you for.

Some couples have lost their marriages because of this tendency to avoid talking about the hard stuff and sugarcoating issues in the name of protecting the other person. True love calls for communication and honesty in good and bad times. That is how a strong connection between partners is made.

Chapter 4: How To Stop Being a Toxic Husband and Become a Healthy and Loving Spouse

The good thing is that you can change and become a better partner and save your marriage. To do this, read on below:

1. Practice Self-awareness

To be self-aware is to have a conscious knowledge of the different aspects of self, including behavior, character traits, and feelings. It is a psychological state in which, when you assume, you become the focus of your attention. This way, you see yourself clearly, exactly as you are, for who you are, not according to the false airs and identities that we either give ourselves or are given by other people.

According to experts, a person who can see themselves clearly makes sounder decisions, builds stronger relationships, and communicates more effectively. This is because they know who they are and what they believe in— and therefore are very clear on who they are not.

You are less likely to be swayed between identities when you know who you are as an original. It is easier to make sound decisions because you are not relying on external influence or the half-baked lies that your brains cook up.

Self-Awareness for Battling Toxicity

How does this help with combating a toxic personality?

- *It Connects You With The Incorruptible and Good Inner Person*

As I mentioned before, none of us is born toxic. We are originally very healthy individuals – clean slates. Most of what we become afterward is influenced by the people around us, the environment we are exposed to, and the circumstances we deal with.

For instance, your parents raise you to respect other people, which becomes something you identify with and believe in. However, you grow up and get with friends who believe that you have to put others down to be superior. They make you believe that the harder you step on people, the more submissive they are and the more of a 'king' you become.

You do it once and then on repeat and enjoy the feeling, mostly because they cheer you on. You do it on repeat until it becomes a character. Remember, this is not who you are, and deep down, there is a feeling telling you that it's wrong. There is a deep-seated discomfort about how you treat people, but since its fun and what your friends recognize as power, you do it anyway.

A self-aware person will recognize and validate this feeling as their own and get the message behind it, which is "This is so not who you are!!!"

If you are not keen on self-awareness, you will believe your friends when they tell you that the feeling is just fear and that you should man up, not be a chicken.

- *It Helps You Get Better at Self-Control*

When you are consciously aware of who you are, it's not just about the good stuff. You also know the vices and the not-so-good stuff that are a part of you, which can be by nature or learned.

- For instance, having a short temper. Being consciously aware of this fact puts you in a better place to be in control. You know your triggers and possible reactions, and therefore, you can avoid the triggers and become more mindful of how you react.

  Say you disagree with your partner and they are saying or doing things that are setting off your temper. You know not to allow yourself to be triggered into a reaction you will regret. You consciously step away and cool off with a simple "Please, I need some air. I promise we shall talk about it when we cool down."

- Another example is for a person who believes they are good and can't be anything but good.

It can be hard for this person to take responsibility for the wrongs that they have done and would rather shift blame. Blaming others comes naturally and is mostly unconscious.

When this person becomes conscious of their behavior and perhaps the feelings that lead them to act this way, they are better placed to practice self-control and make the right decision – biting their ego and taking responsibility.

Bottom-line

Self-awareness will help you get to stay in touch with yourself and your innermost feelings and traits. From this will arise a higher level of consciousness to keep you from rising through life and your relationships on autopilot, doing things the way you are used to without thinking.

This will help you become more 'awake' and intentional. This way, you can catch all those 'unconscious' reactions, actions, and behaviors that are toxic, which you may have learned or practiced so long they became part of your 'autopilot' programming. You will be able to stop, allow yourself to think, and make decisions that are true to your promise of love and that favor your marriage.

2. Cultivate Empathy

The only reason why a person can be mean or abusive to another that they claim to love is a lack of empathy as an individual. Empathy is the key ingredient that makes the difference between a healthy and happy union and a toxic one. You don't want to leave it out, otherwise hurting each other and being mean becomes a norm.

Many people will not give empathy any importance. They have reduced it to be just a 'touchy-feely' thing that some may believe a 'macho' man shouldn't have.

What Exactly Is Empathy?

Simply put, empathy is the ability to put yourself in someone else's shoes. When someone tells you, 'Put yourself in my shoes,' what they are trying to say is 'see this from where I stand,' 'try to feel the way I am feeling.'

In other words, they are asking you to understand as closely as possible what is going on in their mind and heart at that particular moment.

Empathy is experienced in three parts;

i. **Cognitive Empathy** – this is about the mind. It allows us to have a mental experience of another person's experience – to imagine how they must be feeling and say 'that must be tough.'

ii. **Emotional Empathy** – this involves the 'heart' and our feelings. It allows us to go deeper and actually feel what they are feeling even though we may not have the same experiences – or react the same way to similar experiences. Certainly, this doesn't happen to you (or does it?).

When watching romcoms or sad stories, do you feel you can relate to a character's emotions and feel the tears stinging, heart sinking, or palpitating in joy? Now that's emotional empathy.

iii. **Compassionate Empathy**: This is a combination of the two types above. It balances them out; you know, the mind and the 'heart' influencing each other so that we can take what is called empathetic action, a vital part of marital empathy. This makes it a work of the mind, heart, and behavior.

An Example of What Empathy Looks Like in Marriage

You come home tired and hungry, needing a meal and rest. It's just you and your spouse at home. They managed to get off work early, and you find them slumped on the couch, taking a nap. They did not make anything to eat, yet they always do.

The first thing reaction as a normal hungry and tired human being is to get mad at them. You will be asking questions like, "I told you I was coming home, told you I was starving, and here you are slumped on the sofa. Did you even think about me?"

Your spouse explains that they meant to fix dinner early, but they accidentally dozed off.

As an empathetic spouse what do you do?

You listen to them and try to understand how they are feeling without judging. Even though the hunger is biting and you can still feel some anger, you allow yourself to feel the frustration they are feeling right now. I mean, anyone can just doze off after a long day when the body is demanding rest.

Out of compassionate empathy, you tell them that you understand that they were tired too, and they should not worry or feel guilty. You suggest that you could help each other make a meal or better yet, since you are all tired, order take out.

Tell me, how do you think your spouse will feel? They will feel loved, appreciated, and pampered. They will feel that they have a man who cares for more than himself and who understands. It is going to earn you brownie points.

On the flip side, if you weren't so empathic, you might find yourself accusing each other of not caring enough for the other and getting caught up in a toxic fight that your marriage doesn't need.

Choose empathy, always. Please note that it is not something that you are born with, which you can say some have and others lack. Empathy is a skill that you can learn.

How To Become An Empathetic Husband

"I am not a touchy-feely person. How do I show empathy?"

If this is a question you are asking now, this part is for you. Explained below are four steps that can help you learn how to be empathic in mind, heart, and actions towards your spouse;

i. *Listen Emphatically*

We all know how to listen, don't we? The answer is no. Most of us do not have a clue. Our idea of listening is hearing the words flying out of another person's mouth and into our ears and begetting an immediate reaction of words flying out of our own mouths in response.

In the end, we are just exchanging words, everyone saying what they want to say, but no one can really hear the other. There is no communication, just a toxic war of words.

Empathic listening helps us communicate better, understand each other and connect with the other person. For this, we listen not to judge, not to fix, and not to retort. In your head at that moment, you are trying to find the appropriate response. You are listening with the words going to your brain and to your heart, soaking in.

To listen emphatically means that you listen closely to your partner, to understand their feelings, in the same way you would be listening to an instructor teach you how to fly an airplane. Yes, that seriously.

ii. Offer Validation

Being there to listen, nodding as if listening to a sweet musical, is not enough. Validating their feelings, views, and perspectives is very important.

You may listen and be thinking, "Wow! I would not be anxious about stuff like that." Remember, in empathy there is no judgment. Therefore, you should avoid listening and judging your partner's feelings based on how you would handle or perceive a particular situation. We have different ways of interpreting things, which should be acknowledged and respected in a healthy union.

This is what you do instead; validate. First, acknowledge to yourself that these are their feelings (not yours) and that they have the right to feel that way, regardless of what you may think.

Next, respond verbally with words legitimizing/validating their feelings. For example, "I can see why you would feel excited/sad/frustrated about that," "Wow! That must have been exciting news!," "Geez, that must have been scary!"

iii. Share

We are not talking about your opinions. Share in your partner's emotional response. I know how this sounds; getting angry or crying because your spouse is crying, crazy, right? We are not suggesting that you roll on the ground and wail if your partner is doing so. Also, we are not asking you to play pretend – this is toxic too.

You can share in your partner's emotional response if you truly put yourself in their shows, look at the world through their eyes at that moment and allow yourself to experience any part of their emotions. It may not be as easy initially; it will take effort on your part, especially if they are reacting to a situation in a way that you wouldn't. However, the more practice you put into it, the better you will get.

P.s. Do not pretend to feel the anger, frustration, or excitement or whichever emotion – no fake facial expressions, please! If you cannot reflect it, use words like "I can imagine how you feel" and mean it.

Use affection; rub their back, hold their hand, give a congratulatory or comforting embrace where appropriate, and so on. You would rather not share emotion and skip to the next step than pretend.

iv. Action

This step is for responding based on what you have gathered from the previous steps. Here you are supposed to respond in compassion. If you can connect with your spouse emotionally and understand their mind and heart, you will be better placed to know what they need in that particular situation.

This may not be the time to try and 'fix' their problem. Sometimes your intervention may not be needed. At that moment, they may only need an empathetic ear and a compassionate response.

How do you know which one is needed?

Ask. Once they know you are paying attention, it won't be so hard to get an answer. Just ask something like this, "honey, would you want me to listen and help you figure out a solution, or would it be helpful to listen and try to understand?

You can add a reassurance of your commitment to be there. "You know I am here for you, whatever you need." – it will go a long way.

3. Be Intentional About Being a Healthy Partner

You got married to a partner you believed you were in love with, settled down, and life continued rolling.

You joined the cluster of married men, perhaps became a father, and life went on, a day after another, and there are more days to come.

So how are you living as a husband?

What kind of a partner are you?

How does your spouse feel about being married to you?

I mean, do you ever stop to ask these questions – to check in on your role as a lover and husband to another human being?

If you do not, then you have fallen into a routine and are living your marriage on autopilot, you know, just flowing with the flow, doing the things that worked 5 years or 5 months ago and without a clue if they are still effective.

To be fair, everyone falls into a routine. However, toxicity will creep into your marriage if you fall too much into a groove and perhaps become complacent.

You may become the toxic disconnect in the relationship without being conscious about it. Without realizing it, you may stop being the loving husband; you may stop paying attention to your partner, spending quality time, listening and validating them, doing the nice little things that kept the romance alive and so on.

However, if you become intentional about the health of your relationship and being a healthy and loving partner, you can save your marriage from falling into a toxic abyss.

What Does it Mean to be Intentional?

Being intentional is about bringing a commitment, focus, and attention purposefully to something important to you. When you are intentional, you bring a clear purpose and structure to your goals. You align your thoughts, behavior, and actions to match that purpose. It helps you become more present and become more productive to achieve bigger and better goals.

Being Intentional In Being a Healthy Partner

A big part of being intentional is knowing why you choose to do what you do and why you don't do what you do. You see, each one of us is faced with dozens of choices. Since you cannot do everything all at once, you have to choose what to do and what not to do, where to be and where not to be, and so on.

As a husband, you can either be conscious about those choices or move on autopilot and do whatever is possible at that moment, regardless of whether it helps you become a better partner or not. Being conscious takes effort, and many people find it easier to go with the flow and not think about the options.

Being intentional means that you should already be aware of your goals, what you want to do, and why. This will help you go through the options and make your choices wisely– to favor your goals.

For example, your wife is upset about something that you think is too trivial. You could brush it off, go on about your business and leave her to get over it, or you could sit down with her and listen to her pour her heart out.

If your goal is to be a loving husband who is empathetic and emotionally supportive, the choice is clear. Despite what you think or feel, you will sit and offer her an ear and shoulder to lean on.

Why Be Intentional?

Because this is how wonderful and happy marriages are made. No one has ever drifted to a happy union. But when in every moment before you do or say something, you stop to ask yourself, "how am I going to be a healthy and loving partner at this moment?," you are well on your way to creating marital bliss. It leaves no chances open for unconscious toxic behaviors to grow when you are not 'looking.'

4. Ditch Your Ego

The ego makes you a self-important person obsessed with maintaining a certain image, being right, being admired, and getting their way. An egotistical person will do anything to feed and defend their ego. They will go as far as demeaning others, blaming others, becoming defensive, lying, and attacking others for things that don't make any sense just to defend their position.

An egotistical husband will never admit to mistakes, consider or validate their partner's feelings, or take responsibility for their actions. It will always be their ego above their partner and even their marriage.

If you want a healthy and intimate union with your partner, you have to let go of your ego. You see, relationships come with good things, but there are also challenges, and both of you will fall short from time to time. It is important to learn to admit mistakes, take responsibility, ask for and offer forgiveness, and set aside our own selfish needs to care for and support our partners.

This you cannot do if you are all about preserving your ego. However, if you understand that your life and your marriage are not just about you, you can set the ego aside.

When you do, you will find yourself more relatable and understanding to your partner and other people. When you are no longer focused on being defensive, you will be more capable of connecting and having deeper intimacy and fulfillment in your marriage.

5. Allow Yourself To Be Vulnerable

There is no way you will be able to connect with your partner more deeply and intimately (as is needed for a healthy union) if you have all these high walls built around you. There is no connection or intimacy if you are impenetrable.

Many men grow up and learn from society that a man is required to be bold, brave, and strong. In some communities, showing emotion is considered weakness. These inherited beliefs about what a man should or shouldn't be have turned many good men into toxic beings, building up walls so they can be macho.

Why would you want to burn your marriage to live up to some inherited standards?

Showing vulnerability is not a weakness, whether for a man or a woman. It breaks the barriers and bares your heart and soul to your significant other. It is an expression that you are human, with a heart and feelings, who can feel joy and experience sadness.

You are a normal person with normal human weakness who can feel overwhelmed and defeated and need support. You are normal with faults just like everyone else; a person who can make mistakes, identify with another person's feelings, and so on.

What does this vulnerability tell your partner?

It tells them that you are like them, a normal human being just like them. Wondering how this helps? Let me explain.

It is human nature to desire to be around people who we feel are on our level, people we can relate with and share our good news and bad news with without feeling awkward. We love to be around people we do not have to fear, people we can be ourselves around and who do not make our imperfections look like defects. And when we open our hearts and share the not so pretty parts of ourselves, we want to know that we are not the only ones sharing or who are imperfect.

If you are in the habit of trying to act superior and play god; if you keep pretending to be perfect like you cannot do wrong and like everything is always well in your camp, no mishaps and nothing ever goes wrong; if you deny other people's feelings and never open up unless you are trying to portray yourself as a hero, then you tell us that you are not one of us.

You tell us that you are some kind of god, perfect in all ways, a person who has no idea what it is like to be human. We fear you, which you may interpret as respect, but really, we fear you because we cannot trust you. We hate that we have to pretend around you, and we loathe your company. After all, you are not human, right?

However, when you are vulnerable, it tells us that you are one of us. It is easy to open up, bond, and develop a deeper connection. It tells us that we can trust you and that you trust us, and we vibrate on the same level.

You can be our confidant and our friend. We can be imperfect and stupid and be simply human around you. In a marriage, this helps build friendship, foster connection, and deepen intimacy. This is crucial in the building of a healthy union with healthy partners.

6. Open Communication Works

If you want to be a healthy partner, you must learn the art of communication. There is no healthy relationship without communication. Even if it was good initially, if you do not learn to talk about things openly, then it may get really toxic somewhere along the way. Let me tell you why;

There are two constants in our lives; God and change. People evolve; they change, and it's normal. You are not the same people you were on your wedding day by the time you get to your second anniversary. You have grown and changed as individuals and partners.

Communicate to Stay Updated

What may have worked for you two years ago may not work for you today. Your preferences may have changed for various reasons, including new responsibilities, new wants, growth, pain, and so on.

For instance, maybe when you first got married, you had a plan to keep your wild side alive and not become just another boring couple. Then, your idea of doing this was to go on date nights in places with bright lights and blaring music– because you both loved that party life and dancing.

Two years in, you just don't feel that vibe anymore. Your ideal date night is to go to a nice quiet place and sample out their cuisine, look into your partner's eyes and hold hands while having an intimate conversation. Or maybe you have more responsibilities at work or at home (kids, maybe?), and you simply want to rest, stay home, have a nice warm meal, and cuddle on the couch watching your favorite show ('you' refers to either partner).

This change may occur for one partner. If they feel that they can talk about it to you openly, without fear of judgment or being misunderstood, then you can be able to figure out what to do next, which will work for both of you.

However, if open communication is not a thing in your marriage, this little change could create so much trouble and destabilize your union.

Your partner may force themselves to come along to the party nights but hate every moment they spent with you there. They will start to resent you because it seems like you cannot just get it, and you make them do things they don't want to do.

Also, they may not want to come anymore. They start to make excuses about why date nights cannot happen. It's either work or the kids or some headache. Then you will start to think that they do not want to spend time with you anymore, maybe they have fallen out of love or don't find you fun – or there could be someone else…

The assumptions will be endless, and then there will be a disconnect and then what. Toxic behaviors and actions start to creep in just because you couldn't talk about it!

This is why you should have open communication in your marriage, to avoid misunderstandings like this. At least become a person she can talk to openly without fearing your reaction or judgment.

By having open communication with your partner, you are providing a space where both of you can talk about your feelings, concerns and address any changes and other issues. This way, you get to be on the same page and work out solutions together – which is a healthy and powerful place to be as a couple.

7. Show Love

Often, we love our partners on our terms, the way we want to be loved, or the way we think they need to be loved. If you do this, there is a chance that you will get it wrong all the time, and your partner will never feel loved by you – and then you will say that they do not appreciate it, no matter what you try to do.

Each one of us has a love language. There is a way that we understand love and specific things or acts that speak love to us. Several love languages have been identified, including **quality time, gifts, touch, words of affirmation,** and **acts of service.**

All are nice, and a person can identify with all of them. However, there is always one or two that make them feel the most loved. If you identify this, you have found a way into your partner's heart and soul.

Therefore, if you want to be a loving husband, stop trying to love them the way you think they want to be loved. Study your partner, have a candid conversation about love, and let them tell you what they perceive as love.

Please note that this may change over time. Maybe today they feel loved the most when you gift them something nice. A few months later, all they may want is quality time. For this reason, it is important to keep the conversation about love going so that your acts of love can stay relevant.

Trust me; there is no better gift in marriage than to be loved just the way you need to be loved. It's heavenly and fulfilling. It is part of the happily ever after everyone dreams about.

8. Do Unto Your Partner What You Would Like Done To You

Lastly, treat them in the same way that you would love to be treated – with dignity, respect, and love, I hope. If you would not like to be judged, do not judge them. If you would not like to be criticized, blamed, abused, mistreated, demeaned, put down, controlled, gaslighted, then you should never put your loved one in a position where they have to take it.

If you would not like it done to you, do not do it to your partner. Before you can do or say something, assume their position and step into their shoes for a moment. Ask yourself, "how would I feel if someone was doing this to me?"

If you would not like it, then don't do it.

Conclusion

It doesn't matter who you have been in the past and the state of your marriage right now. You have the power in your hands to turn it all around for the better. Yes, you can do it.

The fact that you have read this book means you are willing to change things around. And now, you have an idea of where to begin and what to change to bring positive change in yourself as a husband and in your marriage.

Take action now, and I promise you that happily ever after is a reality you will start to live in.

Good luck!